D0518210

Fact Finders®

Ancient Egyptian Civilization

Pharaohs and Dynasties of Ancient Egypt

By Kristine Carlson Asselin

Consultant:
Jennifer Houser Wegner, PhD
Associate Curator, Egyptian Section
Penn Museum, Pennsylvania

CAPSTONE PRESS
a capstone imprint

Fact Finder Books are published by Capstone Press,
1710 Roe Crest Drive, North Mankato, Minnesota 56003
www.capstonepub.com

Library of Congress Cataloging-in-Publication Data
Asselin, Kristine Carlson.
Pharaohs and dynasties of ancient Egypt / by Kristine Carlson Asselin.
    p. cm. — (Fact finders. Ancient Egyptian civilization)
Includes bibliographical references and index.
ISBN 978-1-4296-7631-1 (library binding)
ISBN 978-1-4296-7979-4 (paperback)
1. Pharaohs—Juvenile literature. 2. Royal houses—Egypt—History—Juvenile literature. 3. Egypt—
Kings and rulers—Juvenile literature. 4. Egypt—Civilization—To 332 B.C. —Juvenile literature. I.
Title. II. Series.

DT83.A875 2012
932—dc23   2011033942

Editorial Credits
Brenda Haugen, editor; Juliette Peters, series designer; Svetlana Zhurkin,
    photo researcher; Laura Manthe, production specialist

Photo Credits
Alamy: North Wind Picture Archives, 25; Art Resource, N.Y.: ©The Trustees of the British Museum,
19, Borromeo, 12; The Bridgeman Art Library: ©Look and Learn/Private Collection/Peter Jackson,
4, National Geographic Image Collection/Herbert M. Herget, 9, Photo ©Christie's Images/Private
Collection/Reginald Arthur, 22; Capstone: Peter Wilks, 11; Corbis: Gianni Dagli Orti, 18, National
Geographic Society, 21; Mary Evans Picture Library, 15, 17; Newscom: akg-images/François
Guénet, 6, 10; Shutterstock: artform, cover (hieroglyphs used throughout book), Fedor Selivanov,
hieroglyphs used as design element throughout book, GSK, cover (statue), javarman, 16, Kharidehal
Abhirama Ashwin, 28, Matej Hudovernik, 29, Mikhail Dudarev, pyramids image used as design
element throughout book, Rafa Irusta, papyrus used as design element throughout book, R-studio,
cover (gold texture); Superstock Inc: Christie's Images Ltd., 26

Printed in the United States of America in Brainerd, Minnesota.
102011   006406BANGS12

TABLE OF CONTENTS

Note to readers:

The years in parentheses after a pharaoh's name are the years that pharaoh ruled Egypt.

Important Discovery

Imagine a powerful king who talks with the gods. If the gods are angered, everyone in the country is punished. The fate of the people rests on the king's shoulders alone.

an Egyptian king at a festival

On the banks of the Nile River in 1897, **archaeologists** discovered a 5,000-year-old **artifact** called the Narmer Palette. Carvings of a powerful king overpowering an enemy decorate the ceremonial plate. At the same time, archaeologists discovered an ancient weapon called a mace. Detailed carvings of royal life appear on the mace head. These artifacts are two of the earliest examples of recorded history. Together they tell of the beginning of a civilization. This civilization survived for thousands of years under the leadership of godlike kings called pharaohs.

archaeologist: scientist who studies how people lived in the past

artifact: an object used in the past that was made by people

Call Me Nesu

The Egyptian word for king was *nesu*. The word *pharaoh* is Greek. The origin of the word pharaoh is *per-aa*, meaning "great house." This term for palace became the term for king around 1450 BC. The ancient Egyptians did not use the term pharaoh.

Ancient Egyptians believed King Osiris civilized the land around the Nile River. Myths told of his talent for teaching the people to make bread and wine. He created the first laws. But his brother, Seth, wanted to be king. He killed Osiris to take the throne. Osiris' only son, Horus, avenged his father's death by defeating Seth and taking his rightful place as pharaoh. All pharaohs who ruled Egypt considered themselves descendants of Horus. The ancient Egyptians worshipped their pharaohs as rulers descended from gods.

Pharaohs protected their kingdoms by keeping order. If a pharaoh failed, ancient Egyptians believed the world would fall into **chaos**. Chaos often meant war with enemy nations. But it could also be a natural disaster or anything that caused widespread misfortune. The fate of the ancient Egyptians' world rested on the pharaoh's shoulders.

The pharaoh was the human link between the gods and people. The gods gave pharaohs their power. The pharaoh communicated with the other gods through offerings, **rituals**, and the building of temples.

The people believed that their pharaoh's efforts brought blessings from the gods. Because of the leadership of more than 170 pharaohs, the Egyptian civilization, which began around 3000 BC, lasted more than 3,000 years.

chaos: total confusion

ritual: an action that is always performed in the same way

Chapter 1

Pharaoh:
The Destiny of Egypt

More than 5,000 years ago, two kingdoms sprang up along the Nile River and struggled for power. The Egyptian **monarchy** began when these two kingdoms united under one ruler. The first pharaoh is often called Narmer. The Narmer Palette and mace head tell the story of how the first pharaoh came to power.

The pharaoh ruled as the head of the government, the leader in times of war, and the chief priest of each god's temple. The pharaoh had complete control over his subjects. But only certain people were born to be pharaoh.

monarchy: a system of government in which the ruler is a king or queen

Family Rule

The title of pharaoh was usually handed down from father to son. But royal wives and daughters played important roles in how a pharaoh came to power. A pharaoh often had several wives. Only one was considered the Great Wife. The Great Wife's children were the **heirs** to the throne. If she only had daughters, the son of another wife could become pharaoh. But that son had to marry a daughter of the Great Wife, one of his half-sisters. Sometimes a pharaoh would invite his heir to rule with him as a co-ruler. Most often pharaohs were male, but at least three women ruled Egypt.

Queen Nefertiti and King Akhenaten honor a favored subject.

heir: a child who has been or will be left a title, property, or money

A crook and flail were symbols of power for a pharaoh.

As a god-king, the pharaoh commanded power and resources over all of Egypt. When a pharaoh wore the ceremonial symbols of the position, the people believed the god Horus was speaking. A pharaoh's symbols included a crook and flail. The crook, similar to a shepherd's staff, symbolized the king as the shepherd of the people. The flail looked like a whip and symbolized supreme power.

The myths of ancient Egyptians were a main part of their history and religion. Egyptians believed their most legendary gods were the first pharaohs. The myths of Ra the sun god and Osiris the god of the afterlife were models for all pharaohs to follow. And each pharaoh was thought to be the human form of Horus, the falcon god and son of Osiris, and ruled for life.

afterlife: the life that begins when a person dies

Many Crowns

A pharaoh had several crowns, each with a different meaning. A white crown represented Upper Egypt in the South. A red crown referred to Lower Egypt around the Nile delta. Worn together, the crowns symbolized a united Egypt.

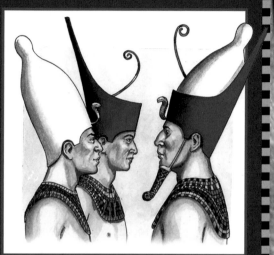

FACT

A cobra ready to strike an enemy was pictured on the front of the king's crown. A king was often shown holding weapons. These weapons were symbols of his job of maintaining order, which included keeping the land safe from invaders.

King Tutankhamun's tomb

Upon accepting the throne from the previous pharaoh, the new pharaoh had an important first job. The new pharaoh was responsible for burying the pharaoh he or she replaced. It took three months and a team of workers to prepare the body and put final touches on the tomb.

The pharaoh's next important duty was to keep away chaos. Chaos in ancient Egypt often took the form of foreign enemies. To protect his people from enemies, a pharaoh made offerings to the gods to keep Egypt in their good favor. Ancient Egyptians believed these offerings not only kept enemies away, but also caused the Nile to flood. An annual flood ensured a bountiful harvest and order for Egypt.

The pharaoh also made important decisions about laws, trade, and relationships with foreign countries. If the pharaoh did not succeed at his tasks, the people believed the gods would be angry and punish Egypt.

On more than one occasion, a pharaoh failed to maintain order. When that happened, the government collapsed. It sometimes took many years to rebuild the government. During times of government collapse, a different family—called a dynasty—took control of the throne.

FACT

Today's scholars disagree about the order of some of the pharaohs and family dynasties. Over time, the record keeping was disorganized, and some records have been lost.

Chapter 2

The Royal Families of Egypt

The ancient Egyptians did not use a traditional calendar. But they did mark the seasons. They also counted the years a pharaoh ruled. They marked the passage of time by counting the dynasties. In 3,000 years, 32 dynasties and 170 pharaohs ruled Egypt. Historians group these dynasties into three time periods—Old Kingdom, Middle Kingdom, and New Kingdom. Between each kingdom, hundreds of years of unrest gripped the country. Pharaohs ruled during those times, but they were weak leaders who did not unite the people. Only strong leadership could re-establish order.

Narmer

The Old Kingdom

The earliest kings of the Old Kingdom ruled before records of family dynasties were kept. Narmer united Upper and Lower Egypt. His story is captured in **hieroglyphs** on the ancient Narmer Palette and mace head. Narmer's reign marks the beginning of a united Egypt.

The Old Kingdom (2625–2130 BC) is considered the golden age of ancient Egypt. During these early dynasties, pharaohs had the Great Pyramids built. Art, building design, and writing flourished. Pharaohs had great wealth and power. But the good times did not last. Years of little rain caused **famine** across the country. Local governors struggled for power after the death of King Pepi II. The Old Kingdom ended in unrest.

FACT

The Great Pyramid was made of 2.3 million stone blocks. Each block weighed between 2.5 and 15 tons (2.3 and 13.6 metric tons).

hieroglyph: a picture or symbol used in the ancient Egyptian system of writing

famine: a serious shortage of food resulting in widespread hunger and death

Famous Pharaohs of the Old Kingdom

The Old Kingdom begins with the fourth dynasty. The Pharaoh Khufu (2589–2566 BC) is best known for building the Great Pyramid at Giza. It was the largest pyramid. Until the 19th century, the Great Pyramid was the tallest structure in the world. Khufu's family members were known for being great builders. Khufu's father, Snefru, and Khufu's son Khafre also built pyramids.

Khafre's pyramid at Giza

Pepi I, the father of Pepi II

Pepi II (2278–2184 BC) was the longest ruling king in history. Pepi became pharaoh when he was 6 years old. While Pepi was a child, his mother, Ankhnesmerire II, and uncle Djau probably served as **regents**. Pepi reigned for 94 years, living to be about 100 years old. He was known for starting new relationships with foreign countries. He was the last pharaoh of the sixth dynasty and of the Old Kingdom.

regent: a person who rules a country when the king or queen is too young to do so

The Middle Kingdom

After the disorder at the end of the Old Kingdom calmed, the Middle Kingdom (2040–1782 BC) began. A family of strong leaders came back into control and re-established order. During these dynasties, written language became more coordinated. Several important texts were written. New technology led to bronze-working and pottery. New inventions included looms used to weave cloth. New musical instruments were also invented.

Mentuhotep II

Famous Pharaohs of the Middle Kingdom

The Middle Kingdom saw several famous pharaohs rise to power. Mentuhotep II (2061–2010 BC) united Egypt and drove enemy forces out of the country. His family is credited with starting the Middle Kingdom.

Amenemhet I (1985–1955 BC) took the throne from a pharaoh who had no heir. He became the first pharaoh of the 12th dynasty. He moved the capital of Egypt from Thebes in the south to Itj-tawy in the north.

Queen Sobeknefru (1799–1794 BC) was one of the few female rulers of Egypt. There are few records of her rule. Scholars believe her husband had been pharaoh and that she came to power after he died. As a female pharaoh, she was respected in the same way as a male king.

During the last dynasty of the Middle Kingdom, pharaohs didn't last long. These short reigns weakened the power of the throne. In time the Middle Kingdom failed because enemy forces overthrew the government and gained power. Invaders took over Lower Egypt and crowned themselves kings.

When the enemies were finally defeated by a dynasty of warrior kings, Egypt reclaimed the throne. The pharaohs of this time built manned forts in northern towns to protect Egypt. The New Kingdom was born.

The New Kingdom

The New Kingdom (1550–1069 BC) spans nearly 500 years of Egyptian history. With their power and wealth, the pharaohs of this time truly were almost godlike people. They left behind art, treasures, and themselves—as mummies. During this time, king's tombs were cut into desert rock cliffs in the Valley of the Kings. The mummies of many kings of the New Kingdom have been found in these tombs.

Famous Pharaohs of the New Kingdom

One of the most famous pharaohs of the New Kingdom was Queen Hatshepsut (1473–1458 BC). She took power after her father Thutmose I. Hatshepsut dressed like a king and even wore a false beard. During her rule, Egypt flourished with new building projects. She also expanded trade with other nations.

During their reign, Akhenaten and Nefertiti (1352–1336 BC) brought new ideas to Egypt. As king and queen, they rejected the old Egyptian traditions. Akhenaten embraced a new god—Aten—who was shown as a falcon with a sun on its head.

Most people today know the name King Tut. King Tutankhamun, or King Tut, (1336–1327 BC) is famous because of his tomb. The discovery of this tomb in 1922 gave archaeologists a peek inside the pharaoh's world.

Queen Hatshepsut

Rameses II (1279–1213 BC) was known as Rameses the Great. He lived to be 96 years old and is rumored to have had 200 wives and more than 100 children. He had two main queens, Nefertari and Istnofret, who were the mothers of his heirs. Ramses was known for his building projects and his wars to keep Syria out of Egypt.

FACT

Each pharaoh had five names. A pharaoh's first name was given at birth. The other four were official titles given to the pharaoh when he or she claimed the throne.

Viziers were often with a pharaoh to help him when needed.

Pharaohs lived very different lives than the common people. Servants woke the pharaohs in the morning. They bathed and dressed the pharaohs before breakfast. Black paint called kohl was painted on the pharaohs' eyelids, and gold pendants hung around their necks. Pharaohs were often carried in a chair by servants.

Egypt's pharaohs had absolute authority over everything and everyone. But they also had help. Educated assistants carried out the pharaoh's wishes. They also helped run the palace's day-to-day activities. The king's main assistants were called **viziers**. They helped make decisions.

vizier: an important government official

The pharaoh was the high priest in every temple across the country and led important rituals. But the pharaoh could not be in all the temples all the time. In the pharaoh's place, other priests handled the daily activities in the temples. They helped organize festivals and led religious rituals.

Ancient Egyptians spent most of their lives preparing for the afterlife. The pharaoh prepared for his own death by creating a resting place for his body. Not all kings built pyramids. In fact, the largest and most famous pyramids were only built during the fourth dynasty. Later pharaohs preferred hidden tombs.

After death, a pharaoh's body was prepared for the afterlife. The body was **mummified** and buried with everyday objects needed for a happy life. These objects often included weapons, jewelry, furniture, and games. Some pharaohs were even buried with their horses and chariots.

mummify: to preserve a body with special salts and cloth

Chapter 3

The End of the Pharaohs

The Egyptian civilization lasted longer than any other civilization in history. Its art and culture affected other societies as they developed in the ancient world. Eventually foreign powers invaded the Nile valley.

The rulers of dynasties 22 through 24 came from Libya, though their families had lived in Egypt for generations. Nubian kings conquered Egypt and ruled during dynasty 25. In 332 BC Alexander the Great of Macedonia marched into Egypt. He defeated the Persians, who had conquered Egypt in dynasty 27. The Egyptian people considered Alexander the Great their rescuer.

As the new ruler of Egypt, Alexander made a **pilgrimage** to the temple of Amon. Because it rained during his trip, he believed the gods of Egypt blessed him. Alexander established the city of Alexandria. It quickly became the center of art, culture, and business in Egypt. Most of the money made in Alexandria at the time was through the export of Egyptian goods.

pilgrimage: a journey to a holy place for religious reasons

After Alexander died, a series of kings named Ptolemy ruled for the next 300 years. These kings started with Ptolemy I (305–285 BC) and ended with Ptolemy XV. They worked hard to keep Egypt powerful. During their rules, new building projects were built, including amazing temples and the great library at Alexandria. When the Roman Empire started gaining power, the conquerors set their eyes on wealthy Egypt.

FACT

Nectanebo II, who died in 343 BC, was the last pharaoh born in Egypt.

Old Alexandria

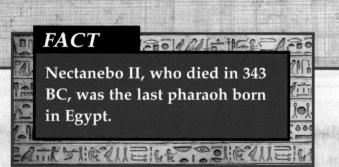

Cleopatra VII

Cleopatra VII (51–30 BC), Egypt's last true pharaoh, came to power as a teenager. Rome was conquering most of the Mediterranean by this time. In an effort to unite Egypt with a powerful ally, Cleopatra became close to Roman general Julius Caesar. Under Cleopatra's reign Egypt prospered.

When Caesar was killed, Cleopatra had a relationship with another ally—Marc Antony. He was a popular general with his Roman soldiers and the people of Egypt. But senior Roman leaders lost faith in Marc Antony. He lost several important battles, which made them doubt his loyalty to Rome. With Cleopatra, Marc Antony had wanted to rule over half the known world. In the end, both Cleopatra and Marc Antony died while in power.

After Cleopatra's death, Egypt became a Roman colony. The title of pharaoh was still used. Roman emperors dressed as pharaohs and carried out the ancient rituals.

Even in ancient times, many of the temples and monuments were world famous. But after Christianity became common, temples were closed or converted to churches. Many statues of gods and other artifacts were destroyed. The ancient Egyptian culture faded. Over thousands of years, desert sands buried ancient Egypt.

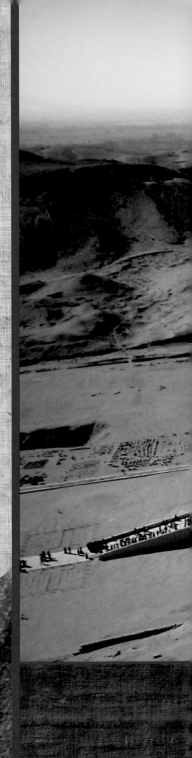

Pharaohs with direct links to the gods do not rule Egypt anymore. But archeological discoveries have uncovered their way of life. Historians have been able to piece together an order for pharaohs based on lists found in tombs and ancient writings. But there are still many missing pieces, and experts sometimes disagree. It has not stopped modern storytellers from drawing on the legacy of ancient Egypt for books, movies, and video games. The pharaohs of ancient Egypt continue to influence the world.

Valley of the Kings
and the temple of
Queen Hatshepsut

FACT

The order of the pharaohs' reigns comes from lists found in tombs. The order also comes from the writing of an Egyptian priest named Manetho. He lived during the reign of Ptolemy II. Because some of the lists exclude whole dynasties, historians are unsure if every pharaoh is now known.

GLOSSARY

afterlife (AF-tur-life)—the life that begins when a person dies

archaeologist (ar-kee-AH-luh-jist)—scientist who studies how people lived in the past

artifact (AR-tuh-fakt)—an object used in the past that was made by people

chaos (KAY-os)—total confusion

famine (FA-muhn)—a serious shortage of food resulting in widespread hunger and death

heir (AIR)—a child who has been or will be left a title, property, or money

hieroglyph (HYE-ruh-glif)—a picture or symbol used in the ancient Egyptian system of writing

monarchy (MON-ahr-kee)—a system of government in which the ruler is a king or queen

mummify (MUH-mih-fye)—to preserve a body with special salts and cloth to make it last for a very long time

pilgrimage (PIL-gruhm-uhj)—a journey to a holy place for religious reasons

regent (REE-jent)—a person who rules a country when the king or queen is too young to do so

ritual (RICH-oo-uhl)—an action that is always performed in the same way

vizier (vuh-ZEER)—an important government official

Adamson, Heather. *Ancient Egypt: An Interactive History Adventure.* You Choose. Mankato, Minn.: Capstone Press, 2010.

Dell, Pamela. *Hatshepsut: Egypt's First Female Pharaoh.* Signature Lives. Minneapolis: Compass Point Books, 2009.

Lunis, Natalie. *Tut's Deadly Tomb.* HorrorScapes. New York: Bearport Publishing Co., 2011.

Surget, Alain. *The Time of the Pharaohs: Great Story & Cool Facts.* Half and Half. San Anselmo, Calif.: Treasure Bay, 2008.

INTERNET SITES

FactHound offers a safe, fun way to find Internet sites related to this book. All of the sites on FactHound have been researched by our staff.

Here's all you do:

Visit *www.facthound.com*

Type in this code: 9781429676311

Super-cool stuff!

Check out projects, games and lots more at
www.capstonekids.com

INDEX